W9-AMO-014

Per

Inventions and Discoveries

Personal and Household Items

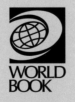

WORLD BOOK

a Scott Fetzer company

Chicago

www.worldbookonline.com

World Book, Inc.
233 N. Michigan Avenue
Chicago, IL 60601
U.S.A.

For information about other World Book publications, visit our Web site at **http://www.worldbookonline.com** or call **1-800-WORLDBK (967-5325).**
For information about sales to schools and libraries, call **1-800-975-3250 (United States),** or **1-800-837-5365 (Canada).**

Editorial:
Editor in Chief: Paul A. Kobasa
Project Manager: Cassie Mayer
Editor: Jake Bumgardner
Researchers: Cheryl Graham, Karen McCormack
Content Development: Odyssey Books
Writer: Rebecca McEwen
Manager, Contracts & Compliance
 (Rights & Permissions): Loranne K. Shields
Indexer: David Pofelski

Graphics and Design:
Associate Director: Sandra M. Dyrlund
Manager: Tom Evans
Coordinator, Design Development and Production:
 Brenda B. Tropinski
Designer: Matthew Carrington
Contributing Photographs Editor: Clover Morell

Pre-Press and Manufacturing:
Director: Carma Fazio
Manufacturing Manager: Steven K. Hueppchen
Production/Technology Manager: Anne Fritzinger

Picture Acknowledgments:
Front Cover: © Ivan Barta, Alamy Images
Back Cover: © Mary Evans Picture Library/The Image Works

The Advertising Archives 31; © Krys Bailey, Alamy Images 23; © Mark Boulton, Alamy Images 29; © Kinn Deacon, Alamy Images 19; © Jeff Greenberg, Alamy Images © ICS/Alamy Images 33; © SPP Images/Alamy Images 21; © Jochen Tack, Alamy Images 19; AP Wide World 43; Atari 42; © Bridgeman Art Library 12, 14, 20; © Museumslandschaft Hessen Kassel/Bridgeman Art Library 7; © Stapleton Collection/Bridgeman Art Library 15; © Victoria & Albert Museum/Bridgeman Art Library 6, 14; © Peter Willi, Bridgeman Art Library 12; © Getty Images 41; © AFP/Getty Images 21, 27, 40; © William Thomas Cain, Getty Images 35; © Hulton Archive/Getty Images 10; © Keystone/Getty Images 25; © Time & Life Pictures/Getty Images 29; Granger Collection 10, 27, 30, 37; © The Image Works 22; © Mary Evans Picture Library/The Image Works 38; © SSPL/The Image Works 8, 11, 16, 17, 18, 22, 26, 32, 36; © Kirby 37; © Hangauer/Kissinger/Levi Strauss & Co. 30; NASA/Space Telescope Science Institute 13; © Kayte M. Deioma, PhotoEdit 4; © Michael Newman, PhotoEdit 35; © Susan Van Etten, PhotoEdit 34; © David Young-Wolff, PhotoEdit 7, 9, 39; © Shutterstock 7, 17, 25, 33, 43, 44; © Smithsonian Institution 28; Museum of Science and Industry, Chicago (WORLD BOOK photo by Chris Stanley) 24.

All maps and illustrations are the exclusive property of World Book, Inc.

Library of Congress Cataloging-in-Publication Data

Personal and household items.
    p. cm. – (Inventions and discoveries)
  Includes index.
  Summary: "An exploration of the transformative impact of inventions and discoveries that led to the development of common personal and household items. Features include fact boxes, sidebars, biographies, timeline, glossary, list of recommended reading and Web sites, and index"–Provided by publisher.
   ISBN 978-0-7166-0390-0
   1. Inventions–Juvenile literature. 2. Technology–Juvenile literature.   I. World Book, Inc.
 T48.P464 2009
 609–dc22
                    2008045637

Inventions and Discoveries
Set ISBN: 978-0-7166-0380-1
Printed in China
1 2 3 4 5 12 11 10 09

▶ Table of Contents

There is a glossary of terms on pages 45-46. Terms defined in the glossary are in type **that looks like this** on their first appearance on any spread (two facing pages).

▶ Introduction

What is an invention?

An invention is a new device, new product, or new way of doing something. Inventions change the way people live. Before the car was invented, some people rode horses to travel long distances. Before the light bulb was invented, people used candles and similar sources of light to see at night. The invention of farming allowed people to stay in one place instead of wandering in search of food. As people established villages and invented ways to travel to other villages, trade (the buying and selling of goods) flourished. Technological advances soon produced a great variety of new goods, services, and capabilities. Inventions continue to shape our world today.

Even the most common household items, such as knives and eating utensils, are inventions.

Inventions in Personal and Household Items

There are many items in our everyday lives that we take for granted, from the jeans we wear to the toothbrush we use to clean our teeth. But how did these personal and household items come to be? In some cases, they came from the work of one person. In many others, they evolved over time, eventually becoming the items we know today.

Throughout history, people have invented tools to make everyday tasks easier. In prehistoric times, for example, people made sharp-edged stone tools that they could use as cutting devices. Such tools later developed into forks and knives.

Over thousands of years, human beings perfected their toolmaking techniques. They mastered the use of fire and discovered new materials for use in building and toolmaking. They passed along this knowledge to future generations.

People have used this knowledge to make a variety of personal and household items. Some are items people use every day, such as eyeglasses that correct vision or wristwatches that keep time. Others make household chores easier and faster, such as vacuum cleaners that help us clean floors and **microwave** ovens

A CLOSER LOOK

Between 35,000 years ago and 10,000 years ago, prehistoric human beings called **Cro-Magnons** lived and hunted in Europe. The Cro-Magnons made dramatically better tools than any people who had lived before them. These tools included harpoons (arrow-shaped weapons), fish spears, and bone needles used to sew clothing made from animal hides. They even created some of the first artwork, carving sculptures out of ivory, bone, and clay.

that can cook food within minutes. Still others offer entertainment, such as board games or **electronic** video and computer games.

Nearly every object in our lives has a unique story behind it. With a little investigation, even the simplest objects become fascinating tales of invention and discovery.

▶ Scissors

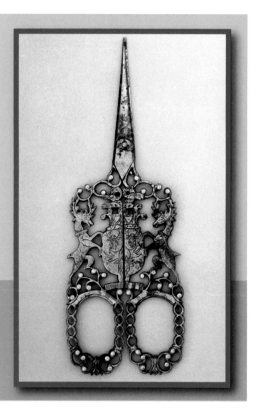

These fancy scissors from the 1700's have been passed down through generations.

More than one million years ago, prehistoric people made the first cutting instruments out of sharpened stones. Over time, people developed such tools as knives. Eventually, they joined two knives together and made scissors.

The Bronze Age began in Mesopotamia in about 3500 B.C., as ancient peoples began to fashion objects from bronze. Bronze is a metal made from copper and tin. These objects included weapons and cutting tools, and eventually, scissors.

These early scissors didn't look much like the scissors we use today. They were more like pairs of tweezers with a C-shaped **spring** at one end, which linked the two bronze blades together. People used these scissors to cut a variety of materials, from human hair to animal hides.

Improvements to scissors came gradually. By about A.D. 100, scissors had blades that crossed over one another and were joined together by a pin or a bolt. Many pairs of scissors, such as those from ancient Egypt, had beautiful decorations on the blades. Others had handles made in fancy shapes. By the 1700's, people were making scissors out of cast (molded) steel. These scissors looked very similar to modern-day scissors.

Scissors use the same kind of force that is used when a person pushes down on a **lever.** When the scissors' handles are pulled apart, the blades open. When the handles

These ancient Roman bronze shears could cut anything from sheep hides to fine cloth.

The long handles on these hedge shears help the person cut through branches.

are pushed together, the blades cut the material at the point where they meet. The cut continues down the length of the blades as they are closed together. Each blade is like a lever, and the bolt is the **fulcrum**—that is, the support on which the lever turns.

Many modern tools have the same basic design as scissors and serve many purposes. For example, pruning shears (long scissors) are used to cut away plant parts, such as branches. Jaws of Life are an enormous, scissor-shaped tool that can cut heavy sheet metal to rescue people who are trapped inside a car after an accident.

A pair of scissors is really two knife blades joined together to form a double lever.

This toothbrush from 1791 looks much like the type people use today.

People have long known about the benefits of dental **hygiene.** As far back as 3000 B.C., ancient people used an early form of a toothbrush called a "chew stick," which was basically a thin twig with a shredded end. A person rubbed the frayed part of the stick against his or her teeth, scraping off food particles and plaque. Some ancient people made toothpicks out of porcupine quills, bird feathers, and even plant thorns.

There were no major improvements to the tooth scraper for more than 4,500 years. Then in 1498, people in China took stiff boar bristles and attached them to bone or bamboo handles, creating the first toothbrush. The bristle brush was introduced in Europe, but people found the bristles to be too firm.

Not all people in Europe brushed their teeth, but those who did used toothbrushes made of soft horsehair. Others cleaned their teeth with a rag or sponge dipped in sulfur (a light-yellow chemical element) or salt to rub their teeth clean. People often attached the rag to a stick to get at their back teeth, which worked more like a tooth mop than a toothbrush.

As early as 1780, people began to build factories to make natural-bristle toothbrushes. **Mass produc-**

tion made toothbrushes much more affordable to the average person, increasing their use.

A big improvement to the toothbrush came in the 1930's with the invention of nylon, a **synthetic** (human-made) material. The first nylon-bristled toothbrushes were sold in the United States in 1938, but they did not become immediately popular. During World War II (1939-1945), American soldiers were issued nylon toothbrushes, and the military encouraged the soldiers to practice good **oral** hygiene. As the soldiers came home, they shared the habit of brushing their teeth with their friends and family. Before long, most people were using toothbrushes.

Early nylon toothbrushes had stiff bristles that often irritated the gums. The American manufacturing company Du Pont corrected this problem in the 1950's, when they introduced the Park Avenue Toothbrush, which had soft nylon bristles. The Park Avenue model sold for 49 cents, a good deal more expensive than the 10-cent hard-bristle model.

Today, there are countless styles of toothbrushes. Electric toothbrushes come with several attachments that thoroughly clean the teeth, gums, and tongue. Traditional toothbrushes have bristles that are specially designed to reach every corner in the mouth. Still, the shape or style of a toothbrush is not nearly as important to dental health as simply using it regularly.

FUN FACT

About 7,000 years ago, Egyptians used tooth powder. Over time, the Egyptians, Greeks, and Romans used a variety of substances, including ox hooves, ashes, burnt eggshells, crushed bones, and pumice, a natural glass formed from volcanoes. These materials were rough on teeth and could wear away enamel, the hard outer layer of a tooth.

Today, many people use electric toothbrushes to thoroughly clean the teeth.

▶ Soap

This illustration from 1771 shows workers stirring vats of soap in a soap factory.

No one knows when or where people first made soap. Its **origins** date back to at least 2800 B.C., when people in Babylonia, a region in what is now southeastern Iraq, created a type of soap made from wood ash and liquid animal fats. Historians believe that they used this soap only for washing clothes.

In the 1700's, Nicolas Leblanc made soap that was affordable to many people.

In 600 B.C. the Phoenicians (*fuh NIHSH uhns*), an ancient people of the Mediterranean coastal areas, were making soap from goat fat, water, and wood ashes. They boiled this mixture to remove liquid from the substance, which created a solid soap.

Though some people may have used soap for cleaning, many others considered it a kind of medicine. The ancient **Romans** are also believed to have used soap, which they called *sapo*. It appears they used it at first for such things as laundry and the processing of animal hides, though not for personal cleaning. The use of soap spread through the Roman Empire. Soap was commonly produced in Italy and Spain by the A.D. 700's.

During the **Middle Ages,** soap production essentially stopped in central Europe. This was mainly due to the Christian church's belief that it was a sin to expose one's flesh, even in the process of bathing. People's lack of cleanliness and dirty living conditions helped contribute to many illnesses, including the **Black Death.**

Some regions made and used soap during the Middle Ages, but it was expensive to produce and often highly taxed by local governments. By the late 1700's, a French scientist named Nicolas Leblanc discovered that lye—a strong kind of salt that cleans things by eating away dirt—could be made from regular table salt. Suddenly soap changed from a luxury item to something that many people could afford to buy. When people discovered in the 1860's that **bacteria** are one of the main causes of disease, soap became widely used.

During World War II (1939-1945), the materials used to make soap became scarce. Companies started making and selling **detergents** made from **synthetic** materials. Manufacturing technology increased dramatically during the war years, and many companies improved the formulas for their detergents.

Today, soap and detergents are produced in the form of bars, flakes, granules (grains), liquids, and tablets. They are used for personal **hygiene,** but they also have many household and **industrial** uses.

By 1900, soaps were made for specific purposes, such as household and laundry use.

▶ The Glass Mirror

Think of all the faces that have been reflected in this gilded mirror from the 1700's.

The Room of Mirrors at the royal palace in Versailles, France, reflects the extravagance of 1600's French royalty.

Prehistoric people noticed their reflections in water and probably thought it was magic. Even after people realized that there was no magic involved, they still wanted to see their reflections. Looking in a calm pool of water was one way to accomplish this, but people slowly developed the technology to make a more permanent and portable mirror.

The first mirrors were made of polished stone or metal, including copper and tin, bronze, gold, and silver. Many ancient peoples, including the Egyptians and Greeks, had them. By the first century A.D., the **Romans** had found a way to make mirrors that were large enough to reflect a person's entire body.

People had discovered how to make glass by 1500 B.C. During the **Middle Ages,** glass manufacture developed in Venice, Italy. Glassmakers there developed a method of making mirrors by spreading a layer of reflective metal on a glass plate.

Venetian glassmakers made the first glass mirrors in 1300, though the reflection in these early mirrors was not clear. While stone and metal mirrors could be sand-polished to create a reflective surface, glass mirrors had to be poured perfectly into a mold the first time. Due to the difficulty of such a task, many early mirrors created blurred or distorted images.

Despite their imperfections, mirrors became a popular form of jewelry among the wealthy in Venice. Men and women wore glass mirrors around their necks as a symbol of their wealth.

Large mirrors, which were used for decoration, also became a symbol of wealth. In the 1600's, the royal palace at Versailles (*vehr SY*), France, was famous for the mirror-lined walls of some of its grand halls and rooms. The mirrors were very expensive to produce—the larger the mirror, the higher the price. They were often framed with ivory, silver, tortoiseshell, or exotic wood.

The French monarchy established its own mirror industry in the late 1600's. Glassmakers in France, including Bernard Perrot, perfected the technique of "casting" glass like metal, which made huge mirrors possible. A mirror nearly 9 feet high was made in 1700.

By the 1800's, people figured out less expensive ways to produce mir-

A CLOSER LOOK

Mirrors have played an important part in astronomy for hundreds of years. In 1616, an Italian astronomer named Niccoló Zucchi invented the first **reflecting telescope.** This type of telescope uses curved mirrors to reflect light and form an image, which people can then study through a lens. The Hubble Space Telescope, operated by the U.S. National Aeronautics and Space Administration (NASA), uses huge mirrors to gather light from distant objects in the **universe** and reflect this light into cameras and computers to analyze the image. The main mirror on the Hubble measures 7.8 feet (2.4 meters) across.

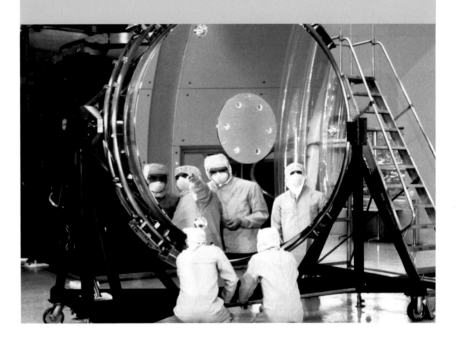

rors, and their price and **prestige** dropped. Many people could now afford mirrors in their homes. Today, most modern homes have at least one mirror and often many more.

▶ The Fork

For most of human history, people have eaten food with their hands. Even after the fork's invention, many people were reluctant to make the switch to using eating utensils. In fact, the fork as we know it today has been in widespread use for only about 400 years.

Before the fork was invented, prehistoric people had long been using knives as weapons or as tools to cut pieces of meat. They most likely made the first knives out of flint and other hard stones and rocks. Later, people began making knives out of bronze or iron.

By the **Middle Ages,** people ate with two knives, one of which was used like a fork to spear food. The first known forks appeared in ancient Greece, but these were used solely to spear pieces of meat from boiling pots. Eventually, two-prong

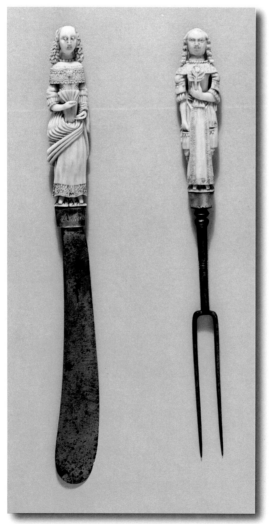

This English ivory- handled knife and fork set is from the 1600's.

forks appeared, which were used to hold down meat while it was carved.

Historians believe that dining forks were first used in the royal courts of the Middle East in the A.D. 600's. Forks had reached Italy by about 1100, but they were not widely used until about 1400. They were used for a variety of foods in France's royal court by the mid-1500's.

The use of forks eventually spread throughout Europe. In 1608, an Englishman named Thomas Coryate traveled to Italy, where he watched with amazement as the people there used a fork to hold meat steady while slicing it, rather than using their bare hands. Throughout Italy, Coryate later

In the Middle Ages, people in Italy enjoyed the convenience of eating with a fork and knife.

By the 1890's, companies offered selections of silver cutlery in a variety of styles and prices.

noted, touching meat with one's hands was considered impolite. In 1611, Coryate published a book about his journeys to Italy and other countries.

At first, forks had only two tines (prongs). As they became more widely used, forks slowly evolved into the form we know today. The tines grew longer, which allowed the food to rest more securely on the fork. The space between the tines grew smaller, so that small pieces of food would not slip through. The number of tines grew from two to four by the 1700's.

Today, forks are used in many countries, though they are not the sole eating utensil. In many Asian countries, chopsticks are used to eat and serve food.

Eyeglasses

Armless spectacles, like these from the 1600's, are called *pince-nez*—French for nose pincher!

Sharp eyesight has always been important to human beings' ability to survive in the wild. But some people are simply born with poor eyesight, while others lose their eyesight as they age. Today, faulty eyesight can be easily corrected with glasses or contact lenses. For prehistoric people, one's eyesight could mean the difference between successfully hunting an animal—or being hunted.

No one is sure who made the first pair of eyeglasses, but many historians believe that they were invented in the 1200's in Italy, which was the center of glassmaking at that time. By the A.D. 1300's, many Europeans were probably wearing glasses.

At first, lenses were not tailor-made to correct the vision of an individual. Instead, shops sold several different types of lenses, which a person would try on and then select the best one. Doctors had not yet created eye charts and tests, so it was up to the person to decide which lens best corrected his or her vision. Early lenses were convex (curved out) and only helped people who had trouble seeing objects that were close-up.

Once the **printing press** was invented in 1440 and books suddenly became more available, glasses were in high demand. By the 1500's, people knew how to make glasses that corrected nearsightedness, which helped people see objects in the distance. Lenses in these early glasses

FUN FACT In the mid-1300's, Italians called eyeglass disks "lentils" because of their circular shape, which resembled the lentil, a popular **legume** in Italy. Eventually, eyeglass "lentils" became known as "lenses."

The Italian artist and inventor Leonardo da Vinci envisioned contact lenses in his sketches in 1508, but the first lenses were not invented until the late 1800's. In 1887 and 1888, Europeans Adolf Eugen Fick, Edouard Kalt, and F.E. Muller, working separately, developed the first glass contact lenses. Hard plastic contact lenses that floated on the tear layer became available in 1948. Soft contacts came to the United States in the 1970's. Early contact lenses were large and fairly uncomfortable, but they improved over time. Today, more than 30 million Americans wear contact lenses.

were made of polished **quartz.** They were set in frames made of bone, metal, or leather straps that could be tied around one's head.

Over the centuries, eyeglasses continued to improve. Lenses became more finely made. By the 1700's, glasses were designed with side-arm pieces that curved behind the wearer's ears, keeping the glasses firmly in place. In 1784, the American scientist and politician Benjamin Franklin invented bifocals, which are two-part lenses that allow people to read type clearly and still see things that are far away.

In the past 100 years, eyeglasses have dramatically improved. In the 1900's, scientists replaced heavy glass lenses with lightweight plastic, which puts less weight and pressure on the nose and ears. Today, eye doctors test patients' vision to figure out exactly what kind of correction they require. Lenses are then custom-made to correct each person's specific eyesight. People also have the choice of wearing contact lenses, which are placed directly on the eyeball to correct vision.

Today, people can choose from virtually any style and color of frames for their eyeglasses.

The Thermometer

Early medical thermometers, like this one from the late 1700's, came with special instructions.

The liquid in Galileo's thermoscope travels up and down the glass neck, revealing changes in temperature.

A **thermometer** is a tool that measures temperature. As the temperature of something changes, other changes happen, too. For example, there may be a change in the object's shape, color, or **volume**—the amount of space it takes up. A thermometer measures one of these changes and usually displays the size of the change as a number.

In the early 1500's, the Italian astronomer Galileo Galilei invented the thermoscope, a device that showed changes in the volume of a substance as its temperature changed. The thermoscope consisted of a glass bulb attached to a glass tube, which was open at one end. The open end of the tube was placed in a dish filled with liquid. As the temperature changed, air inside the tube would expand or contract. This moved the liquid up or down the tube. A person could then estimate the temperature of the air around them based on the length of the thermoscope's air column.

By the mid-1600's, air thermometers were replaced by more accurate instruments called liquid-in-glass ther-

Outdoor thermometers tell us what we already know—what it feels like outside!

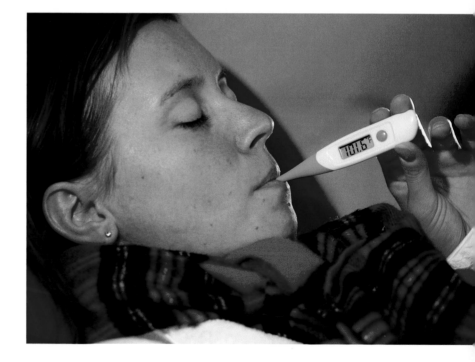

Digital thermometers electronically display temperature readings on a digital screen.

In 1624, the French scientist Jean Leurechon first used the term *thermometre*, which means "measurer of heat."

mometers. These instruments contain a very thin, sealed glass tube partially filled with liquid. As the temperature of the liquid increases, it expands and rises up the narrow tube. A **scale** attached to the tube expresses the height of the liquid column as a temperature value.

In the early 1700's, a German scientist named Gabriel Daniel Fahrenheit first used alcohol, and later mercury (a liquid metal), inside the liquid-in-glass thermometer. Fahrenheit also described a temperature scale. The Fahrenheit scale of measuring temperatures that is used today was named after Fahrenheit to honor his work.

In 1742, the Swedish astronomer Anders Celsius developed the Celsius scale, which was later changed and improved. Though the Fahrenheit scale is more common in the United States, all other major countries of the world use the Celsius scale. Scientists throughout the world also use this temperature scale.

Today, there are many different types of thermometers that can be used to measure all extremes of temperatures.

▶ The Wristwatch

This silver watch from the 1700's chimes the hour.

In today's busy world, keeping track of time is a must. But people in early **civilizations** had no way to keep exact time. Ancient people made **sundials,** which they used to keep track of seasons so they could know when to plant and harvest crops. In the 1300's B.C., the ancient Egyptians developed water clocks that recorded time by measuring water escaping from a container.

People of later civilizations built large mechanical clocks in central clock towers. By the 1400's, people who were wealthy enough to own a clock might have one in their home. But early clocks required constant maintenance to keep accurate time.

According to tradition, the German locksmith Peter Henlein discovered how to build a tiny portable (movable) clock in the early 1500's. He invented a small **spring,** called a mainspring, which powered the clock, eliminating the need for the weights and chains that had been used to power clocks. People in England, France, and Switzerland soon learned how to make watches using the mainspring.

Early watches were heavy, weighing so much that people had to wear them on a thick chain around their neck or hanging from their belt. The clocks weren't very accurate either, and only had an hour hand. During the late 1600's, watchmakers figured out how to add a minute hand. Watches didn't have a second hand until the 1900's.

Over time, people learned how to make smaller and smaller watches. At first, watches were shaped like a small

Peter Henlein

Peter Henlein (1480–1542) was a German locksmith who built the first watch. As a locksmith, Henlein was an expert mechanic. He learned how to work with and craft metal, and eventually became a clockmaker in the town of Nuremberg (*NOO ruhm BEHRG*), Germany. He worked for more than 10 years to figure out how to build a clock that was small enough that people could carry it with them. He finally succeeded in 1510. Henlein's first watches were round and were commonly known as Nuremberg eggs. In his later years, Henlein took care of the church and town hall clocks in his town.

drum. Then they became small enough to fit into people's pockets. Eventually, people could make watches that were small enough to wear on a person's wrist.

When wristwatches were first designed in the late 1800's, they were intended for women. But during World War I (1914-1918), soldiers discovered that it was more convenient to check time on a wristwatch than a pocket watch. From that time on, both men and women started wearing wristwatches.

Watchmaking techniques continued to improve, and watches become more and more accurate. People started building electric watches powered by a tiny battery in the 1950's. In the 1970's, they discovered how to use a **quartz** crystal to keep time in a watch. The quartz watches were amazingly accurate and soon replaced electric and spring-powered watches.

Modern watches can do much more than simply tell time.

▶ The Battery

The Grove battery provided telegraphs with electricity in the 1800's. Its design led to the development of automobile batteries.

In 1799, an Italian scientist named Alessandro Volta made the first working battery. By alternately stacking disks of the metals zinc and silver, and separating each disc with a layer of cloth soaked in a salty solution, he was able to create a device that gave off electric power.

In the decades that followed, people searched for ways to make more effective, reliable batteries. By the 1830's, an English scientist named Michael Faraday had conducted

Many of the tools that people use every day are powered by batteries—devices that use chemicals to create electricity. Without battery power, anything that runs off of electric power would need to be plugged into an electric power source, such as an electrical outlet. Batteries supply power to small devices, such as wristwatches, flashlights, and **cellular telephones.** They also supply power to large machines, such as cars, airplanes, and submarines.

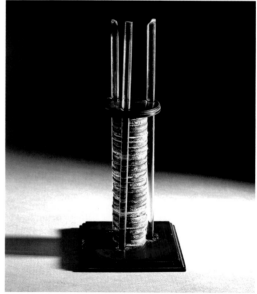

The voltaic pile was the first battery created by Alessandro Volta in 1799.

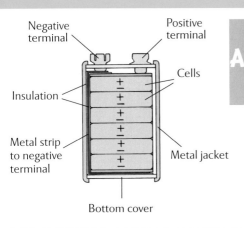

Negative terminal
Positive terminal
Cells
Insulation
Metal strip to negative terminal
Metal jacket
Bottom cover

A battery is made up of one or more units called electric cells. Each cell has all the chemicals and parts needed to make electricity. Battery cells have two structures called electrodes. Each electrode is made of a different chemically active material. The electrodes can be connected to external (outside) terminals. When these terminals are joined by wire, it creates an electric circuit (the path followed by an electric current). This provides electric power to an object.

enough experiments on Volta's early battery that he was able to identify some of the laws, or rules, of how **chemistry** and electric power work together. These laws are still used today in battery technology.

By 1859, people were building batteries that were made out of lead and acid. These batteries could store energy and produce a strong electric current. Modern car batteries are directly descended from this technology.

With each advancement in understanding, scientists learned new ways to improve battery technology, building batteries that were smaller, lighter in weight, easier to charge, and better able to provide steady electric power.

One of the greatest recent improvements in battery technology is the development of **rechargeable** batteries. When the battery runs out of power, a person can simply plug it

into a device that connects to an electrical outlet.

Over the years, scientists have made smaller but more powerful batteries. With these batteries, more kinds of portable, or easy to carry, electric devices can be made.

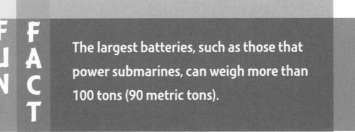

F U N F A C T The largest batteries, such as those that power submarines, can weigh more than 100 tons (90 metric tons).

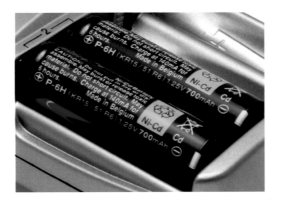

Rechargeable batteries help save both money and the environment.

▶ The Light Bulb

Thomas Edison developed his first incandescent light bulb (above) in 1879.

During the 1800's, people were searching for new ways to use electric power, which they were only beginning to understand. Some experimented with storing electric power in batteries. Others worked to build electric motors. One invention from this period became the very symbol of a good idea: the light bulb.

In the early 1800's, the development of the gas light changed how people lived in big cities in Europe and the United States. In previous centuries, people had relied on candlelight, and then on oil lamps, to provide light after sunset. Cities were now installing gas lighting on city streets. Many homes built during this time had gas pipes that fed lights installed on interior walls. But gas was not the safest source of light, even though it worked efficiently. Gas leaks could poison people. If the leak was large enough, it could cause an explosion.

Because of the gas light's shortcomings, people began developing electric-powered lighting. In 1809, the English inventor Sir Humphry Davy demonstrated his electric **carbon** arc lamp, which used electric power to burn off carbon and produce an intense white light. Later in the century, people started experimenting with **incandescent** light, which uses an **electric current** to heat a coil of wire inside a glass bulb. The coil of wire gives off light when the electric current passes through it.

The American inventor Thomas

Thomas Alva Edison

Thomas Alva Edison (1847–1931) was a famous American inventor. He created useable electric lighting, the phonograph (record player), and the first **power plants** to supply electric power to homes and businesses. Edison got his start in the world of **electronics** when he was only 15 years old. He saved the son of a **telegraph** operator from being hit by a train, and the operator gave Edison lessons in how to operate a telegraph. By 1868, Edison had invented his first machine, an electric vote recorder. He went on to invent countless other machines. Edison also helped found the **motion-picture industry**. His company designed and sold the first commercial machine to show moving pictures.

Edison is usually credited with inventing the light bulb. However, there were at least 20 other inventors who worked to create incandescent light. Edison began working on electric lighting in 1878, and he **patented** a bulb with a carbon filament in 1879. While Edison was working to perfect the light bulb design in the United States, the British **engineer** Joseph Swan built a working light bulb as early as 1860. But Edison envisioned the ways in which electricity would be distributed.

By the early 1900's, many new homes were being wired for electric power. Over time, inventors made improvements to the light bulb.

Today, many countries around the world are switching to energy-saving **compact fluorescent light bulbs (CFL's).** These light bulbs can last 5 to 10 years. By 2010, incandescent light bulbs will be banned (forbidden) in the countries of the **European Union.** By 2012, companies in the United States will begin phasing out most incandescent bulbs.

CFL's burn longer and use less energy than incandescent light bulbs.

These tin cans were used by British soldiers in South Africa during the Boer War (1899-1902).

Canned foods are considered a staple in many kitchens. Because canned foods are processed in a way that preserves the food inside, they can be stored for long periods without spoiling.

The method of preserving foods was developed to fill an immediate need—providing a better way to feed France's traveling armies. Between 1792 and 1795, France was at war with several countries in Europe. Many of France's troops were plagued with hunger and scurvy, a disease caused by lack of vitamin C in the diet. Hoping to find a better way to feed its troops, the French government offered a reward of 12,000 francs to the person who could invent a method of preserving food.

A French inventor named Nicolas Appert set out to meet this challenge. Appert was a former candy maker, wine maker, chef, brewer, and pickle maker. He used his experiences in the food **industry** to his advantage. At the time, people did not know that **bacteria** causes food to spoil. However, as a wine maker, Appert knew that exposure to air spoiled wine. He assumed that the same was true for food, so he boiled the food to remove the air from it.

After 15 years of trial and error, Appert finally developed a successful method to preserve foods. He partially cooked the food, then sealed it inside airtight glass bottles, which were corked. He then dunked the bottles into boiling water.

Appert's preserved foods were tested by French troops for about

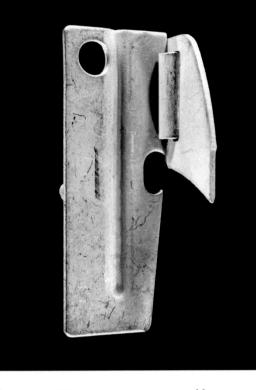

When tin cans were first invented in the 1800's, they were difficult to open. Can openers had not yet been invented, so British soldiers took to opening the cans with knives and bayonets and even shot at them. The first can openers appeared in England in the mid-1800's, but they were difficult to use and could easily cause injury. By 1925, a can opener similar to the ones used today was developed. It had a serrated (toothed) wheel that pinched and rode around the rim of the can.

The tiny P-38 can opener was used by American soldiers in the 1900's. Supposedly, it took 38 punctures to open a can.

four months, and they were all found to be fresh. Appert won the prize for the contest in 1810 and wrote a book about his findings.

Though Appert's method of preserving food was a success, it did have its flaws. The glass bottles were easy to break, a big problem for traveling soldiers. Also, the cork closing on the glass bottles often came off.

An Englishman named Peter Durand decided to make an improved container for preserved foods. In 1810, he **patented** a design for a container made of tinplate (iron coated with tin). The tin coating prevented rusting and corrosion (decay).

By 1812, the first **commercial** canning factory was established in England. A year later, the British military began using the cans for food. By the late 1850's, steel had replaced iron for canning, which made the cans lighter and thinner.

Today, just about every type of food is canned and sold in grocery stores.

The Sewing Machine

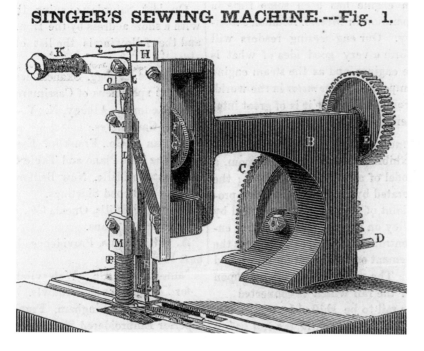

SINGER'S SEWING MACHINE.---Fig. 1.

Singer's foot-powered sewing machine became a fixture in many homes.

Until the mid-1800's, people sewed in very much the same way as their ancestors, although some advances in technology had made the job easier. Instead of sewing with thick bone needles, people used thin, sharp needles made of steel. Instead of using leather threads or cord made out of an animal's gut, people stitched things with thread made from natural fibers, such as cotton or silk. However, sewing was still done by hand, and it required a great deal of time and expertise to do well.

Since the late 1700's, people had tried to build sewing machines. An Englishman named Thomas Saint **patented** a machine in 1790 that could roughly stitch together leather. It had a sharply pointed tool that punched holes in the leather for the needle to pass through. In 1830, a Frenchman named Barthélemy Thimonnier built an early sewing machine that used a hooked needle that made a stitch by passing backward and forward through the cloth.

In 1846, an American mechanic named Elias Howe patented a hand-driven machine that resembles the sewing machines people use today. Howe's machine had a needle with an eye (small hole) at its tip that moved up and down through the cloth. Below the needle was a bobbin (small spool) filled with thread. When the needle pushed the thread through the cloth, a device would loop a line of thread from the bobbin around the top thread, locking the stitch into place. Howe's machine could sew 250 stitches a minute—much faster than any person could sew.

Elias Howe

Elias Howe (1819–1867) was an American inventor who created one of the first practical sewing machines. As a young adult, Howe was sent to learn how to be a machinist—a person who made or repaired machinery. While working one day, he overheard someone say that the first person to invent a working sewing machine would earn a fortune. Howe was inspired. By 1845, he had invented the sewing machine that made him famous. Unable to sell the machine in the United States, Howe took it to England, where he sold the rights to produce it. In 1849, he returned to the United States and had legal battles with other inventors who had profited from the sewing machine of his design.

In 1851, an American inventor named Isaac Singer developed a sewing machine powered by a foot pedal. His machine was efficient and easy for people to use. By 1860, Singer Manufacturing Company was the largest producer of sewing machines in the world.

Today, sewing machines are designed to make all kinds of stitches. They can be used on a wide variety of fabrics, from delicate silk to thick, durable leather. **Electronic** sewing machines have become increasingly computerized, allowing them to perform advanced stitches and functions.

Modern home sewing machines can do a variety of different and complicated tasks.

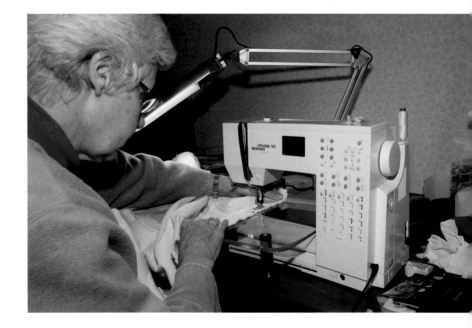

Blue Jeans

The oldest surviving pair of Levi's? These "waist overalls" were made in 1879.

Blue jeans have always been popular with workmen, like these California miners from the 1850's.

Today, blue jeans are a staple of many people's wardrobe. People wear jeans for lounging around, for work, or even for special occasions. But how long have people been wearing jeans, and who first invented them? Though jeans are a big part of modern wardrobes, their story dates back more than 150 years.

In 1853, a 24-year-old **immigrant** from Bavaria (now part of Germany) named Levi Strauss moved to San Francisco, California. At the time, the greatest **gold rush** in United States history was taking place in California, and many people moved

there to take part. San Francisco, the nearest **port,** grew from a small town to a bustling city as people arrived from all over the world.

Strauss had previously lived in New York City, where he worked at his brother's wholesale **dry goods** business. A wholesale business sells large quantities of goods at a time directly to stores. Strauss decided to move out west to open a new branch of his brother's business. Levi Strauss & Co. became a huge success, and

Strauss became known as a smart businessman.

One of Strauss's regular customers was a tailor named Jacob Davis, who often had cloth from Strauss's company shipped to him in Reno, Nevada. Davis had a customer who constantly ripped the pocket seams of his tailored pants, so he set out to find a way to strengthen his pants. He came up with the idea of placing metal rivets (small fasteners) on points of strain, such as pocket corners and at the bottom of the button fly.

Davis's riveted pants became an instant success with **miners** in the Reno area. He decided to sell these new pants **commercially,** but he knew that he needed a business partner. He wrote to Levi Strauss to propose that they go into business together, and Strauss agreed. In 1873, Davis and Strauss **patented** Davis's process of making riveted clothing.

Together, Davis and Strauss soon began making and selling riveted pants out of a brown cotton duck cloth and blue denim. Denim had been traditionally used for workmen's clothing for many years, but the addition of rivets made Levi Strauss & Co.'s clothing tremendously popular among workmen.

For decades, jeans were worn chiefly by outdoor laborers, such as

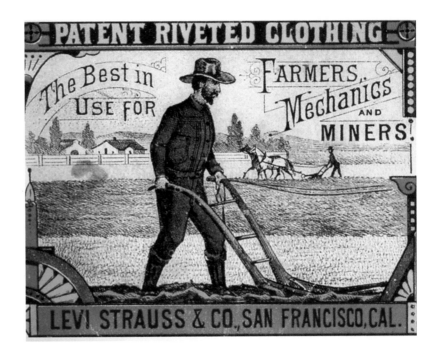

farmers and cowboys. In the 1930's, blue jeans were worn as sportswear by people going to "dude" or vacation ranches out west. By the 1970's, many designers began making a variety of styles for blue jeans. Today, blue jeans are one of the most popular clothing items in the world.

This magazine advertisement for Levi's riveted clothing dates back to the 1880's.

F U N **F A C T** The word *jeans* comes from Genes, the French word for Genoa, a port in Italy. In the **Middle Ages,** working men there wore sturdy cotton pants that were the forerunners of jeans.

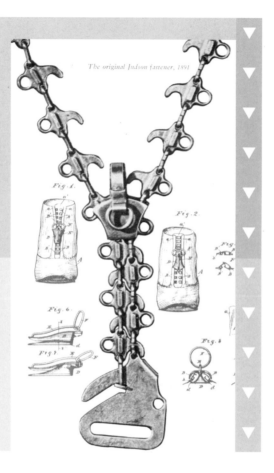

The first zipper, the clasp locker, is shown here in an 1890's advertisement.

I n the late 1800's, an American **engineer** and businessman named Whitcomb Judson invented a simple device that many people take for granted today: the zipper. Judson devised the zipper in order to help a friend with an ailing back who could no longer bend down to tie his shoes.

In 1893, Judson **patented** the "clasp locker," which was a hook-and-eye shoe fastener. Judson brought his new device to the 1893 Chicago World's Fair, but it was largely ignored. By 1905, some manufacturers were using the clasp locker, but the device was not considered practical. The United States Postal Service placed a small order for zipper mailbags, only to abandon them because the zippers frequently jammed.

In 1913, a Swedish-American engineer named Gideon Sundbäck made improvements to Judson's fastener, creating what he called the "hookless fastener." Sundbäck, who worked at Judson's company, replaced the hook-and-eye closure with interlocking teeth that were fastened together by a sliding tab. By 1917, Sundbäck had made additional improvements that made the zipper more reliable.

During World War I (1914-1918), the U.S. army used zippers for clothing and gear. However, the zipper was not yet practical for

By the mid-1900's, people could use an entirely new type of fastener called Velcro for clothing and other accessories. A Velcro fastener consists of two strips that are glued or sewed to the fabrics or other objects to be joined. Tiny hooks made of strong thread cover one of the strips. A fuzzy mat of loops made of thinner threads covers the other. When pressed together, the hooks attach to the loops and form a strong bond. The strips can be easily joined and separated. A Swiss engineer named Georges de Mestral got the idea for Velcro in the 1940's while pulling burs from his trousers and his dog's fur. Today, Velcro is used in clothing, shoes, sports and medical equipment, and inside automobiles and airplanes.

everyday use in clothing. Because early zippers were made of a steel that rusted, they had to be removed prior to washing an article of clothing so they wouldn't rust. Then they would have to be sewn back in when the clothing was dry. People also had difficulty getting used to the new devices. At first, people had to follow an instruction booklet to operate zippers, making them much less convenient than buttons.

Zippers began to catch on after 1923, when the B. F. Goodrich Company made galoshes with Sundbäck's hookless fasteners. B. F. Goodrich himself is believed to have coined the term *zipper*. While demonstrating how his new galoshes could be fastened in one zip, Goodrich made a "z-z-z-zip" sound to emphasize the fastener's ease of use. He even renamed his company's galoshes "Zipper Boots."

By the 1920's, zippers were commonly used in clothing, bags, and footwear. Zippers finally reached the fashion **industry** by the 1930's.

The many interlocking "'teeth" of the zipper give it its strength.

Rubens Crayola crayons were popular with art students in the 1920's. They were named after the great Flemish painter of the 1600's, Peter Paul Rubens.

It is hard to imagine childhood without crayons. However, crayons as we know them today have only been in existence for a little more than 100 years.

A type of crayon was used in Europe by the 1700's, though no one knows when and where it was invented. These early crayons were probably made of charcoal and oil. Later, the charcoal was replaced with powdered **pigments** to give the crayons different colors, and the oil was replaced with wax, which made the crayons sturdier.

In the late 1800's, two cousins in the United States, Edwin Binney and C. Harold Smith, took over a chemical company founded by Binney's father. Their company specialized in **industrial** colorings, such as the pigments that made country barns red and automobile tires black. They also made such goods as shoe polish and printing ink. Later, they began to make slate pencils for students and invented a dustless chalk. Binney and Smith toured schools to sell these items. They soon recognized the need for an affordable, safe, colored crayon for children.

Wax crayons of the time were big, dull-colored, and difficult to draw with. In fact, they were mainly designed for industrial purposes, such as labeling crates and barrels, rather than for use at schools.

Binney and Smith created a new type of crayon by using **paraffin wax** and powdered pigments. Binney's

There is a crayon for every color of the imagination.

Children use crayons to create bright, colorful drawings.

wife came up with the term *Crayola*, which means "oily chalk" in French. In 1903, Crayola crayons were introduced to the market at five cents a box and were an instant success. At first, the box included only eight colors: black, brown, blue, red, purple, orange, yellow, and green. Binney and Smith expanded to 48 per box in 1949, 64 per box in 1958, and 96 per box in 1993.

Today, crayons are sold in countries around the world and come in a variety of colors. Some have special properties, such as fabric crayons, twistable crayons, erasable crayons, and washable crayons.

The Vacuum Cleaner

Herbert Booth's vacuum cleaner worked entirely by suction. It was powered by a loud engine that frightened passing horses.

In the beginning of the 1900's, whole new **industries** sprang up to build electric tools that could accomplish difficult or disliked tasks. One such tool was the vacuum cleaner.

Before the vacuum cleaner was invented, people cleaned their rugs by sweeping off the dirt. If they wanted to get rid of any dirt in the fibers of the rugs, they had to move all the furniture, haul the rugs outside, and then pound out the dirt with a rug-beater. Cleaning was heavy, dirty, and exhausting work.

In the early 1900's, people developed machines that could make cleaning homes easier. An English **engineer** named Hubert Cecil Booth invented a vacuum cleaner in 1901 that was the

size of a horse carriage. In fact, it was pulled by horses and would be parked outside a building that needed to be cleaned while its operators dragged the machine's long hoses into the building. When the house was clean, the group of people who operated the massive vacuum would move it to another house.

In the United States, an inventor named David E. Kenney built a huge vacuum machine that was installed in the cellar of a house and had pipes leading to every room. Hoses attached to the pipes were used in cleaning the room.

The "Little Giant" dust extractor was created by American inventor Hiram Maxim.

The vacuum as we know it today was developed in 1907 by an American janitor named James Murray Spangler, who attached an old fan motor to a soapbox and stapled it to a broom handle. He attached a pillowcase to one end of this machine to catch any dust. By 1908, Spangler had improved his simple vacuum cleaner so much he **patented** it. One of the first vacuum cleaners that Spangler ever sold was to his cousin and her husband, William H. Hoover. The two men ended up forming the Hoover Company, which to this day is famous for its vacuum cleaners.

Sales of the Hoover vacuum cleaner were slow at first, so the company offered a 10-day free home trial. Before long, there was a Hoover in nearly every home, and the problem of rug cleaning was solved.

Today, vacuum cleaners can remove dust and dirt from furniture, woodwork, curtains, and other above-the-floor items. They can dramatically improve living conditions for people with allergies. Some houses have fairly large central, built-in vacuum cleaners. Each room has nozzles and hoses that are attached to ducts (tubes) in the wall. A centrally located vacuum pulls the dirt through the hoses and down the ducts to a single dirt-collecting system.

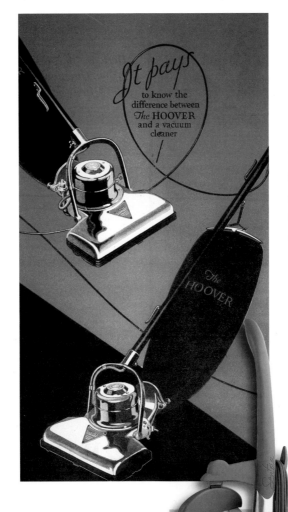

This 1926 advertisement shows the modern style of the Hoover vacuum cleaner.

Modern vacuum cleaners can be used to clean floors, furniture, curtains, and other above-the-floor items.

The Microwave Oven

The microwave "cooker of the future" amazed the public in 1947.

In the 1800's, most people cooked using wood- or coal-heated stoves. Then companies started manufacturing gas stoves and then electric stoves. With each new kind of stove, **engineers** took the features that worked well on earlier versions and added new technology to get the stove to work even better. Many modern kitchens feature large stoves, with gas burners and electric ovens.

Most modern kitchens also have an entirely different sort of machine for cooking food: a **microwave** oven. These electric-powered ovens were first invented in 1947 to heat food in an entirely new way. Traditional stoves heat up the oven and let the hot air soak into the food, cooking it from the outside in. Microwaves, on the other hand, send waves of energy into the food, cooking it from the inside out.

In a microwave oven, the air surrounding the food doesn't heat at all. Instead, any water, fats, and sugars in the food soak in the rays and heat up quickly and intensely. Microwave ovens cook food much more quickly than traditional ovens, but sometimes the food doesn't heat as evenly. There may be sections that are boiling hot, while other parts are still icy. Microwaves can't brown or crisp foods either, so many people choose to use traditional ovens for baking.

The American engineer Percy Spencer was the first person to dis-

A microwave oven has a device called a magnetron that produces microwaves. The waves travel through a metal chamber to the stirrer, which scatters them into the oven. The waves are absorbed mainly by the water **molecules** in food. They cause the molecules to vibrate rapidly. This vibration results in **friction** between the molecules, which in turn produces the heat that cooks the food.

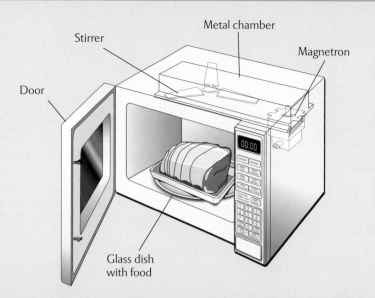

Door

Stirrer

Metal chamber

Magnetron

Glass dish with food

cover that microwaves could heat foods. In the 1940's, he was working to generate microwave radio signals to be used in **radar.** One day, he was standing in front of one of the machines that produced microwaves, and the waves melted a chocolate bar that he had in his pocket. He then tested popcorn by setting it in front of the machine. It quickly started popping all around the laboratory. In 1947, the first **commercial** microwave oven was being built and sold in the United States. But it weighed over 750 pounds (340 kilograms) and so was not suited for home use.

Since the first countertop microwave ovens were introduced for home use in the 1950's, they have changed the way people cook their food. They don't work for every kind of cooking, but they have still become a useful tool in many kitchens around the world.

Today, many people use microwaves for cooking.

▶ Instant Noodles

(ノンフライ麺)

チキンラーメン

Momofuku Ando poses with his famous product at the Instant Ramen Museum in Osaka, Japan.

Throughout the 1900's, people developed foods that could be made faster and more easily than ever before. An early form of instant coffee hit the market in the early 1900's. **Commercial** frozen foods were developed in the 1920's. Then in 1958, a Taiwanese businessman named Momofuku Ando introduced a cheap, fast, and flavorful new food product: the instant noodle.

As a young man, Ando had moved to Osaka, Japan, where he went to school and later founded several businesses that ultimately failed. Soon after World War II ended in 1945, Ando witnessed long lines of poverty-stricken Japanese waiting in the cold for a bowl of hot noodles. Remembering this experience a decade later, he decided to develop noodles that people could prepare themselves quickly and easily.

After working in his backyard shed for a year, Ando arrived upon a method of making noodles by flash-frying them. The noodles could then be rehydrated with boiling water and ready to eat within three minutes.

Ando sold his first instant noodles,

called "Chikin Ramen," in 1958. The noodles were named for their chicken broth flavoring and for the Japanese word for noodles (ramen). That same year, Ando's company changed its name to Nissin Products Co., Ltd.

Ando first tested the noodles at a local shop in Osaka. At first, the noodles were up to six times more expensive than noodles in most Japanese noodle shops. Still, Ando managed to sell 12,000 servings in one year. Their popularity rose when the noodles became cheaper to make and so could be sold at a lower price.

Nissin introduced Chikin Ramen to the United States in 1970. A year later, Ando released his most famous product, Cup Noodles, which came in a waterproof container that people could use as a bowl. Cup Noodles became a big hit in many countries. This allowed Ando's company to lower the price of the noodles even further since they sold them in large quantities.

Today, Nissin is one of the world's leading instant noodle companies, selling about 46 billion servings in 2006 alone. Instant noodles now come in a variety of flavors. They are a favorite among college students or anyone needing a quick, easy-to-make meal.

Today, many companies make instant ramen noodles.

With microwavable instant noodles, all you need are chopsticks—or a spoon.

▶ Electronic Games

Between 1978 and 1992, more than 30 million Atari game consoles were sold.

Beginning in the mid-1900's, several scientists developed a new form of entertainment called **electronic** games, which included video games and computer games. Electronic games grew out of the development of televisions, computer technology, and graphic design **software** that improved throughout the 1900's.

In 1958, an American scientist named William Higinbotham created what some historians consider to be the first video game. Higinbotham worked at the U.S. Brookhaven National Laboratory. There, he developed a video game called *Tennis for Two* as a way to make the laboratory's science exhibit more interactive and engaging.

Tennis for Two was played on a 5-inch (12.7-centimeter) screen, which displayed a two-dimensional side view of a tennis court. Players used controllers to serve and lobby a small tennis ball across the screen. The game was a big hit with visitors to the laboratory.

In the early 1950's, television sets became increasingly popular. A German-born television **engineer** named Ralph Baer wanted to create interactive games that could be played on TV's. At first, Baer's idea was rejected by his employers at a U.S. television manufacturing company where he worked at the time. Ten years later, Baer decided to pursue his idea.

In 1968, Baer **patented** the first video game **console,** called the Brown Box. In 1971, the television manufacturer Magnavox licensed Baer's technology, which they renamed Odyssey and sold as the first home video game console in 1972.

Around this time, the first video arcade games were introduced on the market. In 1971, an American engineer named Nolan Bushnell cre-

A CLOSER LOOK

Some electronic games allow many people to participate in a virtual world using the Internet. These virtual worlds are stored on remote (faraway) computers called servers. Once connected to a server, each player takes on the role of a character in the game. Thousands of subscribers can connect to a game at the same time. Players can meet up with one another to do battle, complete quests, and even shape the world itself.

ated the first video arcade game, *Computer Space.* The following year, he released *Pong,* an arcade game based on table tennis.

The graphics and technology for early video games were simple, but they dramatically improved by the mid-1980's. During this time, the Japanese company Nintendo released the Nintendo Entertainment System (NES) to the international market. Nintendo revived the video game **industry** with the help of its feature game, *Super Mario Bros.,* which showcased bright colors, original music, and imaginative characters.

Throughout the mid- to late 1900's, home video game systems continued to improve. Games became more complicated and graphics more lifelike. The growth of computer gaming began in the 1980's with the spread of **personal computers.** Computers themselves became more powerful, enabling them to handle three-dimensional graphics.

In the early 2000's, social gaming developed. Social games can be played by multiple people at once. For example, *The Sims* is a social game in which players build virtual neighborhoods and guide the lives of their inhabitants. Players can create their own content and share it over the **Internet.**

Home video games are such a huge business that conventions are held many times per year all over the world. Here, a visitor to a convention in Germany plays a golf simulator.

Important Dates in Personal and Household Items

c. 3000 B.C. Ancient Egyptians used chew sticks to clean their teeth.

c. 2800 B.C. Ancient Babylonians began using soap.

c. 1500 B.C. Ancient Egyptians began making scissors.

c. A.D. 100 People in the Middle East made the first large mirrors out of polished brass or silver.

A.D. 600's Forks were used in the royal courts of the Middle East.

1200's The first known eyeglasses were produced.

1200's–1300's Europeans made the first glass mirrors.

1498 The Chinese invented a boar-bristle toothbrush.

Early 1500's Peter Henlein of Germany invented the mainspring to power small clocks.

Late 1500's An early version of the thermometer was invented in Italy.

Early 1700's Daniel Gabriel Fahrenheit of Germany invented the first alcohol thermometer and mercury thermometer.

1700's Europeans made modern-style scissors out of hardened steel.

Late 1700's Nicolas Leblanc of France discovered how to make soap out of lye.

1790 Thomas Saint of England invented a machine to stitch leather together.

1790's Alessandro Volta invented the first battery.

1801 Humphrey Davy of England built the first electric carbon arc lamp.

1846 Elias Howe invented the first modern-style sewing machine.

1860 Joseph Swan of England invented the working light bulb.

1873 Jacob Davis and Levi Strauss patented Davis's process of making riveted clothing.

1879 Thomas Edison introduced the first working incandescent light bulb.

1893 Whitcomb Judson patented the clasp locker.

Late 1800's The first wristwatches were developed.

1901 The first vacuum cleaners were developed.

1903 Crayola crayons were first sold in the United States.

1947 The first microwave ovens were developed.

1968 The first instant noodles were sold in Japan.

1968 Ralph Baer patented the first video game console.

bacteria single-celled organisms that can only be seen using a microscope.

Black Death the bubonic plague that spread through Europe in the 1300's and destroyed one-fourth of its population.

carbon a common chemical element, often found in the form of charcoal or coal.

cellular telephone a wireless telephone that transmits and receives messages via radio signals.

chemistry the science that deals with the characteristics of simple substances (elements), the changes that take place when they combine to form other substances, and the laws of their behavior under various conditions.

civilization nations and peoples that have reached advanced stages in social development.

commercial having to do with trade or business.

compact fluorescent light bulb a small, energy-efficient light bulb that screws into a standard light bulb socket.

console a panel, usually of buttons, switches, and dials, used to control electrical or electronic equipment in a computer, automobile, missile, or other device.

Cro-Magnons prehistoric human beings who lived in Europe, Asia, and North Africa from about 35,000 to 10,000 years ago.

detergent a substance that acts like soap, used for cleansing.

dry goods cloth, ribbons, laces, and similar textile fabrics.

electric current the movement or flow of electric charges.

electronic of or having to do with electrons.

electronics devices that make use of electricity and transistors. Cellular telephones, computers, and televisions are all examples of electronics.

engineer a person who invents, plans, or builds things, such as engines, machines, bridges, or buildings.

European Union an organization of European countries that works for cooperation among its members.

friction a rubbing of one object against another. Friction typically creates heat.

fulcrum the support on which a lever turns or is supported in moving or lifting an object.

gold rush a sudden rush of people to a place where gold has just been found.

hygiene rules of health, the science of keeping well.

immigrant a person who comes into another country or region to live.

incandescent glowing with heat; red-hot or white-hot; heated to such a high temperature that it gives out light.

industry; industrial any kind of business, trade, or manufacture.

Internet a vast network of computers that connects many of the world's businesses, institutions, and individuals.

legume a type of plant with seeds in pods, such as beans and peas.

lever a bar that rests on a fixed support called a fulcrum. One end of the bar transmits force and motion to the other end, much like the action of a seesaw.

mass production the making of goods in large quantities, especially by machinery and with division of labor.

microwave a high-frequency electromagnetic wave, usually having a wavelength from 1 millimeter to 30 centimeters.

Middle Ages the period in European history between ancient and modern times, from the A.D. 400's through the 1400's.

miner one who works in a mine, a large hole or space dug in the earth to get out ores, precious stones, coal, salt, or anything valuable.

molecule the smallest particle into which a substance can be divided without chemical change.

motion picture a series of pictures on a strip of film recording very slight changes in position of persons or things, and projected on a screen at such a speed that the viewer gets the impression that the things pictured are moving.

oral of the mouth.

origin the thing from which anything comes; beginning; starting point; source.

paraffin wax a colorless or white substance, obtained chiefly from crude petroleum (oil).

patent (n.) a government-issued document that grants an inventor exclusive rights to an invention for a limited time; (v.) to get a patent for.

personal computer a computer used by one person at a time.

pigment a coloring material, usually a powder. When pigments are mixed with oil, water, or some other liquid, it makes paint.

power plant a building with machinery for generating power.

prestige importance, based on someone's reputation or known abilities or achievements.

printing press a machine for printing from types, plates, or blocks.

port a place where ships and boats can be sheltered from storms; harbor.

quartz a very hard mineral found in many different types of rocks, such as sandstone and quartzite.

radar an instrument for determining the distance, direction, and speed of unseen objects by the reflection of radio waves.

rechargeable something that can be charged again by being connected to a source of electric power.

reflecting telescope a type of telescope that uses mirrors instead of lenses.

Roman of or having to do with ancient Rome or its people. The Roman Empire controlled most of Europe and the Middle East from 27 B.C. to 476 A.D.

scale a series of marks made along a line or curve at regular distances to use in measuring.

software the designs, instructions, routines, and other printed matter required for the operation of a computer or other automatic machine.

spring an elastic device that returns to its original shape after being pulled or held out of shape. A spring consists of one or more strips or plates, usually of metal, bent, coiled, or otherwise shaped or adjusted.

sundial one of the oldest known devices for the measurement of time.

synthetic human-made.

telegraph an instrument used to send messages by means of wires and electric current.

thermometer an instrument for measuring temperature.

universe everything that exists anywhere in space and time.

volume space occupied, as measured in three dimensions.

▶ Additional Resources

Books:

- *Amazing Leonardo da Vinci Inventions You Can Build Yourself* by Maxine Anderson (Nomad Press, 2006).

- *Great Inventions : The Illustrated Science Encyclopedia* by Peter Harrison, Chris Oxlade, and Stephen Bennington (Southwater Publishing, 2001).

- *Great Inventions of the 20th Century* by Peter Jedicke (Chelsea House Publications, 2007).

- *How to Enter and Win an Invention Contest* by Edwin J. Sobey (Enslow, 1999).

- *Inventing the Future: A Photobiography of Thomas Alva Edison* by Marfe F. Delano (National Geographic Society, 2002).

- *Inventions* by Valerie Wyatt (Kids Can Press, 2003).

- *The Light Bulb* by Jennifer Fandel (The Creative Company, 2004).

- *So You Want to Be an Inventor?* by Judith St. George (Philomel Books, 2002).

- *What a Great Idea! Inventions that Changed the World* by Stephen M. Tomecek (Scholastic, 2003).

Web Sites:

- Elias Howe
  http://memory.loc.gov/ammem/today/jul09.html
  The U.S. Library of Congress's Web page with information on Elias Howe, one of the inventors of the sewing machine.

- Exploring Leonardo - Museum of Science, Boston
  http://www.mos.org/sln/Leonardo
  Focusing on Leonardo da Vinci, this is a useful site for teachers and students in grades 4-8. Includes a helpful section on the elements of machines (the lever, gears) and a discussion of perspective.

- Inventor of the Week
  http://web.mit.edu/invent/iow/i-archive-cp.html
  The Lemelson-MIT program's Web site includes an index searchable by invention or inventor, games and trivia, and links to other sources.

- Kids Pages - United States Patent and Trademark Office
  http://www.uspto.gov/go/kids
  The U.S. Patent and Trademark Office's student Web site includes games, puzzles, links to information about inventions, and a glossary.

- National Inventors Hall of Fame
  http://www.invent.org/index.asp
  Information on inventions and inventors from the National Inventors Hall of Fame.

Index